n

28.50

D1074811

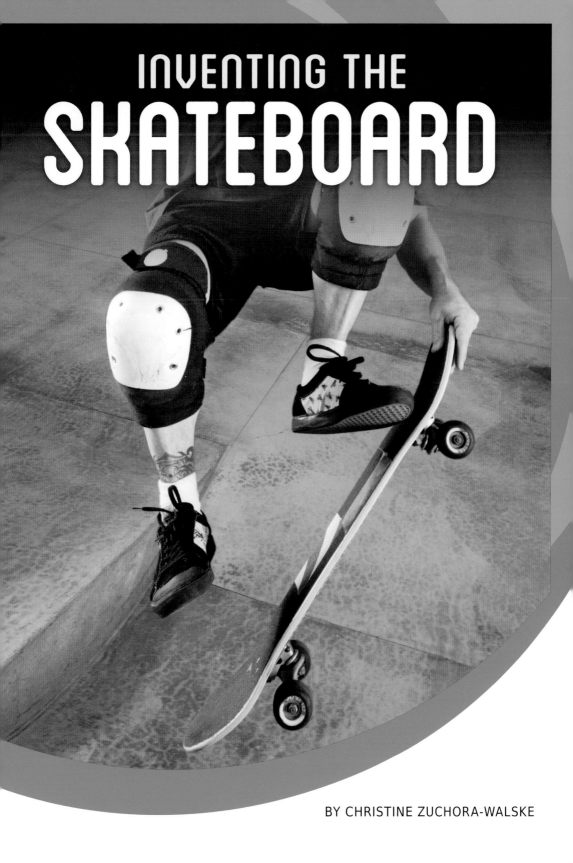

INVENTING THE
SKATEBOARD

BY CHRISTINE ZUCHORA-WALSKE

The Child's World®
childsworld.com

Published by The Child's World®
1980 Lookout Drive • Mankato, MN 56003-1705
800-599-READ • www.childsworld.com

Acknowledgments
The Child's World®: Mary Berendes, Publishing Director
Red Line Editorial: Design, editorial direction, and production
Photographs ©: Shutterstock Images, cover, 1, 6, 8; ClassicStock/Corbis, 4; William
Gottlieb/Corbis, 7; Bettmann/Corbis, 10; SuperStock/Corbis, 13; iStockphoto, 14, 17,
20; Focus on Sport/Getty Images, 18; Heike Brauer/Shutterstock Images, 21

ISBN 9781634074599

LCCN 2015946285

Printed in the United States of America
Mankato, MN
December, 2015
PA02284

ABOUT THE AUTHOR

Christine Zuchora-Walske studied literature, communications, and publishing
at the University of Notre Dame and the University of Denver. She has been
writing and editing children's books and articles for more than 20 years.

TABLE OF
CONTENTS

Chapter 1
ROLLER SKATES AND SCOOTERS......5

Chapter 2
SIDEWALK SURFBOARDS.................9

Chapter 3
BUILDING A BETTER BOARD.............15

Chapter 4
PLASTIC WHEELS...........................19

Glossary 22
To Learn More 23
Source Notes 24
Index 24

ROLLER SKATES AND SCOOTERS

The twins just couldn't get enough of roller-skating. Whenever the brother and sister had a few spare minutes, they laced up and raced off. Most of their friends did, too. It was 1925. Roller skates were all the rage.

The twins' parents smiled. Things had really changed. Roller-skating had been popular when they were young. But at that time, roller skates were fancy gadgets for grown-ups. By 1925, roller skates were common children's toys.

The twins liked to mess around with their toys. And they were getting bored with their roller skates. They felt antsy. They wanted a new adventure.

The sister had an idea. They could pry off their skate wheels. Then, they could attach the wheels to something else. Her brother

◀ A girl straps on her roller skates in the 1930s.

liked that idea. He had seen a kid on a wooden scooter. How about scooters? His sister nodded.

The twins searched the town's alleys. They found two empty crates. Next, they dug in the family's toolshed. They found a hammer, nails, and small sticks of lumber. They turned the crates on their ends. They nailed the sticks to the top ends of the crates. The sticks became handles. The twins nailed the bottom ends of the crates to wooden planks. They put the roller skate wheels underneath the planks.

Now the twins had crate scooters. They zipped along the roads. They flew down hills. They skidded around corners. They raced each other and other kids. Sometimes cheering crowds lined the streets to watch them go.

▲ Early roller skates had wheels made of metal.

▲ A group of boys race their crate scooters on a city street in the 1950s.

But even that grew boring after a while. The kids needed a new challenge. So some of them yanked off the handles. Soon they pried off the crates, too. Now their toys were simple wooden planks on wheels. The kids raced around just like before. But now they had to balance without holding on to anything.

These were the first skateboards. And the twins were not the only ones who thought of it. Kids all across the United States were putting wheels on boards. The story of skateboarding was off and rolling.

Chapter 2

SIDEWALK SURFBOARDS

It was a summer day in 1960. Larry Stevenson squinted at the setting sun. He felt glad the long day was over. It had been very hot in the lifeguard tower. He worked at Venice Beach in California. On sizzling days like this, crowds of swimmers came to the beach. But the surfers had stayed away today. The ocean's waves were too small.

Stevenson climbed down onto the sand. He walked to the parking lot. There he saw a group of surfers. But instead of surfing the waves, they were surfing the pavement. Stevenson tossed his gear into his car. He stopped to watch them.

The surfers rode wooden skateboards. Most were homemade. All were noisy. Each skateboard was a rickety plank with steel wheels from roller skates. "It . . . vibrated on the asphalt enough

◀ **A surfer walks along Venice Beach.**

▲ Children skateboard down a New York
street in the 1960s.

to jar every bone in your body and loosen every tooth,"
described one early skateboarder.[1] But it did look like fun.

Stevenson was a surfer, too. Soon he gave sidewalk surfing a
try. He found that it *was* fun.

Over time, he noticed something. When the sea was flat,
surfers went elsewhere looking for fun. He could see why
some chose skateboarding. It was similar to surfing. But their
skateboards were awful. He thought about this problem. Then he
had an idea.

Stevenson figured he could make skateboarding really take off if he did two things. First, he needed to get more surfers interested in it. He could show them that surfing and skateboarding were similar. Second, he could build better skateboards.

In 1963, he started a magazine called *Surf Guide.* It contained stories about both surfing and skateboarding. The same year, he also started a skateboard company. He named it Makaha after a famous surfing beach in Hawaii.

Stevenson built Makaha skateboards in his garage. They were shaped like miniature surfboards instead of rectangles. They had clay wheels instead of steel ones. Clay was softer than steel. It gripped the ground better and vibrated a little less. So Makaha skateboards rode smoother than other skateboards.

Stevenson formed a skateboarding team. It traveled around and showed off Makaha skateboards. Makaha sponsored the first-ever skateboarding competition at a school in Hermosa Beach, California.

Stevenson's strategy worked. Surfers loved his skateboards. Other surfing companies soon started making skateboards of their own. Some made skateboard decks, or boards, with fiberglass in them. The fiberglass made the boards a bit bendy. These boards steered better and rode smoother than all-wood boards.

Skateboarding soon became very trendy. From 1963 to 1965, skateboard makers sold more than $50 million worth of skateboards.

Then, in late 1965, skateboarding came to a screeching halt. And it wasn't because the trend had passed. The skateboard itself was the problem.

Two teenagers ride their skateboards on a sidewalk. ▶

Chapter 3

BUILDING A BETTER BOARD

"One week I was getting so many orders, people were leaving them on my doorstep," Larry Stevenson recalled. "The next, I was getting seventy-five thousand cancellations in a single day!"[2] What on earth had happened?

By late 1965, skateboarding had swept all the way across the United States. Skateboarding youths were everywhere, from the boardwalks of California to the sidewalks of New York City. Young people everywhere wanted skateboards. Skateboard makers were cranking out skateboards as fast as possible.

But adults were worried. They thought skateboards were dangerous. Doctors called them "a new medical menace."[3]

These people had a point. Companies were too busy making skateboards to spend time improving them. And they really needed improving. These skateboards looked nicer

◀ **An early skateboard**

than homemade ones. But they didn't ride much better. They still shook terribly. And they were still hard to control. A lot of skateboarders fell and were hurt badly. A few even died. Many cities banned skateboarding. People stopped buying skateboards.

Stevenson's skateboard business crashed. He went back to lifeguarding. But he didn't stop thinking about skateboards. He wondered how he could make them better.

In 1969, he came up with a great idea. He added a tail to the rear of the skateboard. The tail was a metal bar shaped into a triangle. The triangle bent upward. The tail acted as a lever. Riders could press down on the tail to lift the front of the skateboard. Now they could turn more easily. They could spin the skateboard. They could even launch it into the air. The tail gave riders more control. It also helped them do more tricks. It became known as a kicktail.

Makaha started making skateboards again, but now the skateboards had kicktails. This perked up other skateboard makers. People began to think about more improvements.

A skateboarder rides low to the ground for better balance. ▶

Chapter 4

PLASTIC WHEELS

In 1970, college student Frank Nasworthy spent the summer with his family. They lived in Washington, DC. He visited a nearby plastics factory called Creative Urethanes, which his friend's family owned. There, Nasworthy noticed a barrel full of roller skate wheels. They were made of polyurethane, a type of plastic. A roller skate company had rejected the wheels. They were up for grabs. "Wow, those would fit on our skateboards," thought Nasworthy.[4] He took a few dozen.

Nasworthy and his friends removed their skateboards' clay wheels. Those wheels never worked very well. They gave a bone-rattling ride. They often slipped on the pavement. They wore out quickly. They could shatter if the rider landed really hard.

The young men put polyurethane wheels on their skateboards. They spent the rest of the summer sidewalk surfing all over Washington, DC. They had a blast. Their new wheels were so much smoother, faster, and sturdier than the old ones.

◀ In the 1970s, people started skateboarding in empty water pipes.

In 1973, Nasworthy convinced Creative Urethanes to make wheels especially for skateboards. Nasworthy's idea caught on. Many other companies started doing the same thing. They attached the new wheels to new **trucks**. A truck is the gear that fastens the wheels to the deck. The trucks were made just for skateboards, not roller skates. With these new trucks, a rider could turn easily. He just leaned in the direction he wanted to go.

The creativity of Stevenson, Nasworthy, and others like them brought skateboarding back to life. Safety gear improved, too. People designed better knee pads, helmets, and wrist guards. Riders could now do amazing things on their skateboards. They could skate up walls, spin, and jump high in the air. Skateboarding grew popular again.

Today, skateboards are popular with both kids and adults. Skateboards are no longer just toys for kids looking for some fun. Skateboarding is a respected sport now. No one knows where the story of skateboards will go next. But one thing is for sure. It won't end anytime soon!

PARTS OF A SKATEBOARD

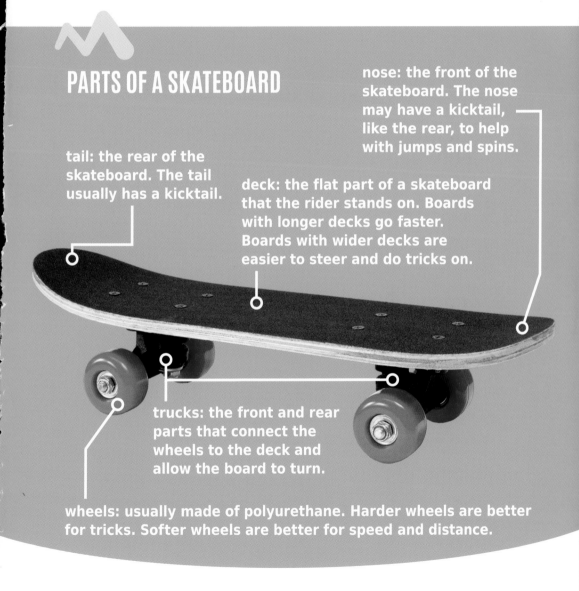

nose: the front of the skateboard. The nose may have a kicktail, like the rear, to help with jumps and spins.

tail: the rear of the skateboard. The tail usually has a kicktail.

deck: the flat part of a skateboard that the rider stands on. Boards with longer decks go faster. Boards with wider decks are easier to steer and do tricks on.

trucks: the front and rear parts that connect the wheels to the deck and allow the board to turn.

wheels: usually made of polyurethane. Harder wheels are better for tricks. Softer wheels are better for speed and distance.

21

GLOSSARY

decks (DEKS): Decks are the flat parts of skateboards. Skateboards' decks look like small surfboards.

fiberglass (FY-ber-glas): Fiberglass is a strong, light material made from glass formed into fibers, or threads. Many skateboard decks have fiberglass in them.

lever (LEV-ur): A lever is a stiff tool that lifts one end when the other end is pressed. A skateboard's kicktail acts as a lever.

menace (MEN-uhs): A menace is something that is dangerous or can cause harm. In the 1960s, many parents thought skateboarding was a menace to children's health.

polyurethane (pah-lee-YUR-uh-thayn): Polyurethane is a type of plastic. Skateboard wheels are made of polyurethane.

sponsored (SPAHN-surd): Sponsored means paid for something. It costs money to hold a skateboarding competition, so a company sponsored the event.

trendy (TREN-dee): Trendy is used to describe something that is very popular or fashionable. In the 1970s, skateboarding was trendy.

trucks (TRUKS): Trucks are pieces of metal that connect a skateboard's wheels to its deck. Trucks are what allow the skateboard to turn.

TO LEARN MORE

Books

Blaine, Victor. *My Skateboard*. New York: PowerKids Press, 2015.

Kesselring, Susan. *Being Safe on Wheels*. Mankato, MN: The Child's World, 2011.

Sandler, Michael. *Gnarly Skateboarders*. New York: Bearport Publishing, 2010.

Web Sites

Visit our Web site for links about skateboards:
childsworld.com/links

Note to Parents, Teachers, and Librarians: We routinely verify our Web links to make sure they are safe and active sites. So encourage your readers to check them out!

SOURCE NOTES

1. Michael Brooke. *The Concrete Wave: The History of Skateboarding.* Toronto: Warwick, 1999. Print. 18.

2. Valerie J. Nelson. "Larry Stevenson Dies at 81; Skateboard Innovator and Publisher." *Los Angeles Times.* Los Angeles Times, 27 Mar. 2012. Web. 15 May 2015.

3. Ibid.

4. Eric M. Weiss. "A Reinvention of the Wheel." *Washington Post.* Washington Post, 17 Aug. 2004. Web. 15 May 2015.

INDEX

crate scooter, 6

Creative Urethanes, 19, 20

fiberglass, 11

Hermosa Beach, California, 11

kicktail, 16

Makaha, 11, 16

Nasworthy, Frank, 19, 20

polyurethane, 19

roller skate, 5, 6, 9, 19, 20

Stevenson, Larry, 9, 10, 11, 15, 16, 20

Surf Guide, 11

surfing, 9, 10, 11, 19

Venice Beach, California, 9